TEAM SPIRIT®

SMART BOOKS FOR YOUNG FANS

30 ► 20 ► 10 ►

THE PITTSBURGH STEELERS

BY
MARK STEWART

NORWOOD HOUSE PRESS
CHICAGO, ILLINOIS

Norwood House Press
P.O. Box 316598
Chicago, Illinois 60631

For information regarding Norwood House Press, please visit our website at:
www.norwoodhousepress.com or call 866-565-2900.

All photos courtesy of Getty Images except the following:
Black Book Partners (4, 10, 19, 22, 23, 25, 29, 35 top right & bottom, 39, 43 both),
Author's Collection (6, 7, 34), SCH Publications (9), SportsChrome (14),
Topps, Inc. (15, 20, 21, 28, 35 top left, 38, 40, 42 both, 45),
Curtis Publishing (16), Time Inc./Sports Illustrated (41), Matt Richman (48).
Cover Photo: Icon SMI

The memorabilia and artifacts pictured in this book are presented for educational and informational purposes,
and come from the collection of the author.

Editor: Mike Kennedy
Designer: Ron Jaffe
Project Management: Black Book Partners, LLC.
Special thanks to Topps, Inc.

Library of Congress Cataloging-in-Publication Data

Stewart, Mark, 1960-
  The Pittsburgh Steelers / by Mark Stewart.
    p. cm. -- (Team spirit)
  Includes bibliographical references and index.
  Summary: "Team Spirit Football edition featuring the Pittsburgh Steelers
that chronicles the history and accomplishments of the team. Includes access
to the Team Spirit website which provides additional information and
photos"--Provided by publisher.
  ISBN 978-1-59953-536-4 (library edition : alk. paper) -- ISBN
978-1-60357-478-5 (ebook)
  1. Pittsburgh Steelers (Football team)--History--Juvenile literature. I.
Title.
  GV956.P57S85 2012
  796.332'640974886--dc23
                                          2012012315

Manufactured in the United States of America in North Mankato, Minnesota.
313R—012018

COVER PHOTO: The Steelers celebrate a long touchdown run in 2010.

Table of Contents

ABOUT OUR GLOSSARY

In this book, there may be several words that you are reading for the first time. Some are sports words, some are new vocabulary words, and some are familiar words that are used in an unusual way. All of these words are defined on page 46. Throughout the book, sports words appear in **bold type**. Regular vocabulary words appear in ***bold italic type***.

Meet the Steelers

There are many ways to measure success in football. For most fans, it comes down to a simple question: How many times has your team won the **Super Bowl**? The Pittsburgh Steelers won their sixth in January of 2009—more than any other team.

The Steelers are likely to add to their record. The team is built to win championships. Each year, a group of good players comes together to play great football. It has been that way for *generations*. No matter who is coaching the team or who the Steelers are facing on the field, chances are they will come out on top.

This book tells the story of the Steelers. Every Sunday they pull on their uniforms and play their hearts out. They hit hard, think fast, and work as a team. Pittsburgh fans expect this and more of the players and coaches, and the Steelers are happy to give them exactly what they want.

Ben Roethlisberger embraces Troy Polamalu after a Pittsburgh victory. They have helped the Steelers win more Super Bowls than any other team.

During the darkest days of the *Great Depression*, the sport of *professional* football was in need of smart, ambitious people. Art Rooney fit that description. Rooney lived in Pittsburgh, Pennsylvania. He was young, loved sports, and had money to spend. Rooney bought a team in the **National Football League (NFL)** in 1933 and named it the Pirates, after the city's baseball club.

"Bullet Bill" Dudley

Rooney had some good players on his team during the 1930s, including Johnny "Blood" McNally, Cap Oehler, Ray Tesser, Armand Niccolai, and Byron "Whizzer" White. In 1940, Rooney changed the name of the team to the Steelers, in honor of Pittsburgh's steel industry. Not until 1942, however, did they have their first winning season.

The star of that team was a **rookie** passer named Bill Dudley. He was small and slow and threw the ball with a weird sidearm motion. Still, he usually found a way to win. Pittsburgh fans loved him. Just when it looked as if the Steelers were ready to contend for the NFL championship, Dudley and many teammates were called away to fight in *World War II*.

When Pittsburgh's stars returned, the game had changed, and the Steelers were slow to keep up with the times. At one point, the team went eight years in a row without a winning season. During the 1950s, Pittsburgh had a strong defense that featured Ernie Stautner, Dale Dodrill, Bill McPeak, Jerry Shipkey, and Jack Butler. But they lacked a great runner and passer. The Steelers could have had the two best players of the *era*—running back Jim Brown and quarterback Johnny Unitas. But the team decided not to **draft** Brown and cut Unitas during training camp.

The Steelers began to show improvement in the late 1950s and early 1960s. They were led by quarterback Bobby Layne, running back John Henry Johnson, and receiver Buddy Dial. It was not until the early 1970s, however, that Pittsburgh fans were finally rewarded with a championship team.

LEFT: When World War II began, Bill Dudley swapped his football jersey for a military uniform.   **ABOVE**: John Henry Johnson signed this photo, which shows him in the early 1960s.

The turning point came when the Steelers hired Chuck Noll as their coach. Noll had played for the Cleveland Browns in the 1950s. He was an assistant coach with the Baltimore Colts in the 1960s. His first job as a head coach was with Pittsburgh.

Noll's coaching *philosophy* was simple. He wanted to stop opponents from scoring. With the Steelers, he built a *dynasty* around a defense called the "Steel Curtain." It starred linebackers Andy Russell, Jack Ham, and Jack Lambert, defensive back Mel Blount, and defensive linemen L.C. Greenwood and Joe Greene.

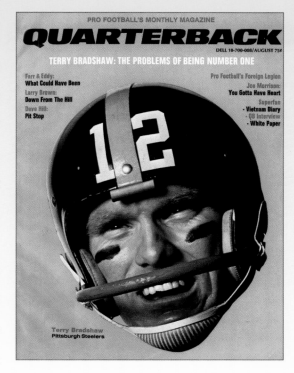

On offense, the Steelers could strike quickly. Quarterback Terry Bradshaw led the way. An excellent group of blockers opened holes for running back Franco Harris. Pittsburgh also had two superb receivers, John Stallworth and Lynn Swann. They could break free from the defense and score from anywhere on the field. The Steelers reached the Super Bowl four times in the 1970s and won it each time.

LEFT: Chuck Noll watches the action from the sideline. He coached the Steelers to four championships.   **ABOVE**: Terry Bradshaw was the quarterback for all four Super Bowls under Noll.

In the years that followed, the Steelers welcomed many more exciting players, including Louis Lipps, Rod Woodson, Neil O'Donnell, Levon Kirkland, Kevin Greene, Kordell Stewart, and Barry Foster. Pittsburgh returned to the Super Bowl in 1996 but lost to the Dallas Cowboys.

Pittsburgh ushered in a new era of success in 2004, after taking Ben Roethlisberger in the NFL draft. The rugged quarterback was strong and confident, and his teammates looked to him for leadership. The Steelers made "Big Ben" their starter as a rookie, and he helped the team go 15–1. The following season, he led Pittsburgh to victory in Super Bowl XL.

The Steelers protected Roethlisberger with a group of good blockers, including Alan Faneca and Jeff Hartings. They helped clear the way for running backs Jerome Bettis and Willie Parker. With a powerful rushing attack, Roethlisberger had time to throw the ball to his favorite receivers, Hines Ward and Heath Miller. The defense starred hard-hitting Troy Polamalu, Casey Hampton, James Harrison, and Joey Porter.

The Steelers won another Super Bowl three seasons later. They survived a string of tough opponents during the 2009 regular season, and then turned it up a notch in the **playoffs**. The Pittsburgh defense that year was as fearsome as any in the NFL. Yet in Super Bowl XLIII against the Arizona Cardinals, it was the offense that made the difference. Roethlisberger hit Santonio Holmes with a picture-perfect pass to win the game.

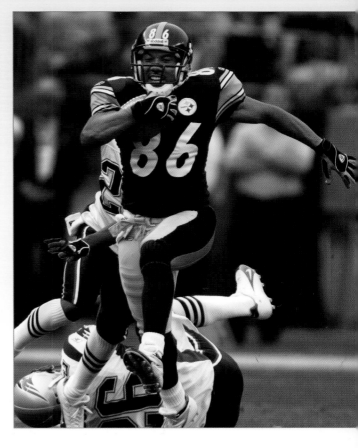

As Roethlisberger grew into a *veteran* star, the Pittsburgh passing attack became even more dangerous. Newcomers Mike Wallace and Antonio Brown joined Ward and Miller to give the Steelers an awesome group of receivers. The team returned to the Super Bowl after the 2010 season, only to lose to the Green Bay Packers. Through it all, Pittsburgh continued the team *tradition* of playing good defense. For many fans, these are the good old days—all over again!

LEFT: "Big Ben" Roethlisberger looks for an open teammate.
ABOVE: Hines Ward breaks into the clear against the New England Patriots.

Home Turf

Throughout their history, the Steelers have played right in the city of Pittsburgh. For many years, they shared a stadium with baseball's Pittsburgh Pirates. First it was Forbes Field and later Three Rivers Stadium.

In 2001, the Steelers moved into Heinz Field. The stadium was designed specifically for football. The University of Pittsburgh football team also plays there.

Heinz Field is shaped like a horseshoe. The open end faces lovely Point State Park. When the wind blows, kickers get very nervous on this part of the field. Sometimes, there's no telling which way the ball will go.

BY THE NUMBERS

- The Steelers' stadium has 65,050 seats.
- The stadium cost $281 million to build.
- Approximately 12,000 tons of steel were used in the construction of the stadium.

The fans bundle up for a winter game at Heinz Field.

Dressed for Success

Gold has been a part of Pittsburgh's uniform for a very long time. Starting in 1940, the team wore all-gold helmets. That changed in 1954 when the Steelers added a black stripe down the middle. Eight years later, they introduced the famous *logo* that is still in use today. It's a circle with three diamonds—yellow, orange, and blue—and the word *Steelers*.

At first, team owner Art Rooney was not sure if he liked the logo. He decided to put it on the right side of the helmet only. When the Steelers won nine games and made the playoffs in 1962, Rooney celebrated by ordering special black helmets. The logo looked great against the black background!

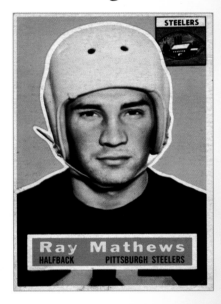

Black has been an important color for the Steelers ever since. Today, they wear black jerseys for home games and white jerseys on the road, always with gold pants. The Pittsburgh uniform is one of the most stylish in the NFL.

LEFT: Mike Wallace wears the team's famous uniform and helmet.
RIGHT: This 1950s trading card shows Ray Mathews wearing Pittsburgh's gold helmet.

We Won!

Pittsburgh fans waited more than 40 years before the Steelers played for their first championship. Their patience was rewarded with four Super Bowl victories in six seasons. Coach Chuck Noll led a powerful team that had amazing talent at every position. Pittsburgh had three **All-Pro** players on the offensive line in Jon Kolb, Ray Mansfield, and Mike Webster. Receivers Lynn Swann and John

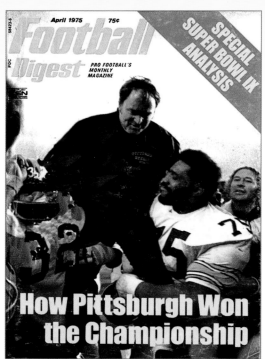

Stallworth, running back Franco Harris, and quarterback Terry Bradshaw were also All-Pros.

The defense was even better. Joe Greene, L.C. Greenwood, Ernie Holmes, and Dwight White controlled the **line of scrimmage**. Linebackers Jack Ham, Jack Lambert, and Andy Russell roamed all over the field to make tackles. Mel Blount, Glen Edwards, Mike Wagner, and Donnie Shell kept the passing game in check.

In their first shot at an NFL title—Super Bowl IX— the Steelers found themselves in a grim defensive battle with the Minnesota Vikings. The difference in the game was Harris, who gained 158 yards. Pittsburgh won 16–6, and Harris was named the **Most Valuable Player (MVP)**.

One year later, the Steelers were back in the Super Bowl. They faced the Dallas Cowboys, and again the game was very close and exciting. Swann was the hero this time. Two weeks after being hospitalized with a **_concussion_**, he made four beautiful catches and scored a touchdown. Pittsburgh won 21–17.

The 1978 Steelers were nearly unstoppable. They breezed through the playoffs and met the Cowboys in a Super Bowl rematch. Bradshaw was the star in a 35–31 victory. He threw two touchdown passes to Stallworth, one to Swann, and another to Rocky Bleier.

17

Pittsburgh's fourth Super Bowl was supposed to be its easiest. The Los Angeles Rams did not have many stars, but they proved to be a tough opponent. In fact, the Steelers trailed in the fourth quarter. But two long passes from Bradshaw to Stallworth—and an **interception** by Lambert—helped Pittsburgh win 31–19.

The Steelers' next Super Bowl victory came at the end of the 2005 season. For more than two decades, the team had struggled to find a great quarterback. In just his second season, Ben Roethlisberger led Pittsburgh to victory in Super Bowl XL against the Seattle Seahawks.

The Steelers took control in the second half after a 75-yard run by Willie Parker put them ahead 14–3. In the final quarter, Roethlisberger handed off to Antwaan Randle El, who caught the Seahawks by surprise when he stopped and fired a long touchdown pass to

Hines Ward. Pittsburgh held on for a 21–10 victory.

Three years later, the Steelers were back in the Super Bowl, this time against the Arizona Cardinals. Pittsburgh scored the first two times it had the ball to take a 10–0 lead. The Cardinals stormed back, but James Harrison intercepted a pass at the goal line and ran it 100 yards the other way for a touchdown. It was the longest play in the history of the Super Bowl.

Arizona didn't quit. The Cardinals moved ahead 23–20 in the fourth quarter. The Steelers had enough time for one final drive. Roethlisberger hit Santonio Holmes with three long completions to get the ball to Arizona's 6-yard line. With 35 seconds left, Roethlisberger fired a pass to the right edge of the end zone. Holmes stretched over the sideline to catch it and kept both of his feet in bounds as he fell to the turf. It was one of the greatest catches in NFL history, and it gave the Steelers their record sixth Super Bowl victory.

LEFT: Antwaan Randle El fires his touchdown pass against the Seattle Seahawks.　**ABOVE**: Ben Roethlisberger and the Steelers are #1 after winning Super Bowl XLIII.

To be a true star in the NFL, you need more than fast feet and a big body. You have to be a "go-to guy"—someone the coach wants on the field at the end of a big game. Steelers fans have had a lot to cheer about over the years, including these great stars …

THE PIONEERS

Ernie Stautner

TACKLE-STEELERS

ERNIE STAUTNER   Defensive Lineman

- BORN: 4/20/1925   • DIED: 2/16/2006
- PLAYED FOR TEAM: 1950 TO 1963

Ernie Stautner was small for a defensive lineman. But no one in the NFL played more aggressively or hit harder than he did during the 1950s.

JOE GREENE   Defensive Lineman

- BORN: 9/24/1946   • PLAYED FOR TEAM: 1969 TO 1981

"Mean" Joe Greene was one of the hardest players to block in NFL history. He was incredibly strong, and no one was quicker when the ball was snapped. Greene was voted NFL Defensive Player of the Year twice.

TERRY BRADSHAW   Quarterback

- BORN: 9/2/1948   • PLAYED FOR TEAM: 1970 TO 1983

Terry Bradshaw came to the NFL with a lot of talent but very little confidence. Not until the Steelers showed they believed in him did he become one of history's best quarterbacks.

JACK HAM   Linebacker

- BORN: 12/23/1948   • PLAYED FOR TEAM: 1971 TO 1982

Jack Ham played behind L.C. Greenwood and Joe Greene on the left side of the Pittsburgh defense. While these two tied up blockers, Ham used his speed to zero in on the ball carrier. On passing plays, he played like a defensive back. Ham made 32 interceptions during his career.

JACK LAMBERT   Linebacker

- BORN: 7/8/1952   • PLAYED FOR TEAM: 1974 TO 1984

Jack Lambert was a great **all-around** player. He stopped runners in their tracks with hard tackles and was quick enough to cover receivers and intercept passes.

LYNN SWANN   Receiver

- BORN: 3/7/1952   • PLAYED FOR TEAM: 1974 TO 1982

Lynn Swann was a fast and *elusive* receiver who had excellent concentration. For many years, he and John Stallworth formed the NFL's best receiving duo.

LEFT: Ernie Stautner
RIGHT: Jack Lambert

ROD WOODSON   Cornerback

- BORN: 3/10/1965
- PLAYED FOR TEAM: 1987 TO 1996

Rod Woodson's daring style tempted many quarterbacks to challenge him. That was usually a mistake. Woodson came back from a terrible knee injury to help the Steelers reach Super Bowl XXX.

JEROME BETTIS   Running Back

- BORN: 2/16/1972
- PLAYED FOR TEAM: 1996 TO 2005

Jerome Bettis gained 1,000 or more yards in each of his first six seasons with the Steelers. He was so difficult to stop that he was nicknamed the "Bus."

HINES WARD   Receiver

- BORN: 3/8/1976
- PLAYED FOR TEAM: 1998 TO 2011

Hines Ward was known for doing it all with the Steelers—catching, running, throwing, blocking, and tackling. He was voted MVP of Super Bowl XL.

JAMES HARRISON   Linebacker

- BORN: 5/4/1978
- FIRST YEAR WITH TEAM: 2002

No team drafted James Harrison because scouts thought he was too small to succeed in the NFL. The Steelers saw something special in Harrison and gave him a chance. He was the team MVP in 2007, and a year later he was named NFL Defensive Player of the Year.

TROY POLAMALU   Safety

- BORN: 4/19/1981   • FIRST YEAR WITH TEAM: 2003

Troy Polamalu developed into one of the NFL's best defenders after he joined the Steelers. His long hair made him easy to spot on the field. Polamalu was the Defensive Player of the Year in 2010.

BEN ROETHLISBERGER   Quarterback

- BORN: 3/2/1982   • FIRST YEAR WITH TEAM: 2004

Ben Roethlisberger led the Steelers to the Super Bowl three times in his first seven seasons. When he beat the Seattle Seahawks for his first championship, he became the youngest quarterback to win a Super Bowl, at age 23. Roethlisberger was at his best when the pressure was on late in games.

LEFT: Rod Woodson   **ABOVE**: James Harrison

Calling the Shots

The Rooney family has run the Steelers since their very first season. After Art passed away in 1988, his son Dan took over the team. Art's grandson Art Rooney II is in charge today.

The Rooneys have always believed that a championship team starts with a strong coach. In the years after World War II, Jock Sutherland turned the Steelers into one of the NFL's most feared defensive teams. In the late 1950s, Buddy Parker put together a roster of experienced players, and the Steelers became one of the league's better teams.

Chuck Noll was the coach who best fit the Rooneys' idea of what a leader should be. Noll had a plan for building a champion and could be very stubborn when it came to his coaching strategy. He did not like to give loud *inspirational* speeches. Instead, he would talk to players quietly and let them know exactly what he expected. Under Noll, the Steelers won 209 games and four Super Bowls.

Pittsburgh's next coach was Bill Cowher. He was the opposite of Noll—he always seemed to be excited about something. The Steelers did not believe in giving star players big contracts, so Cowher

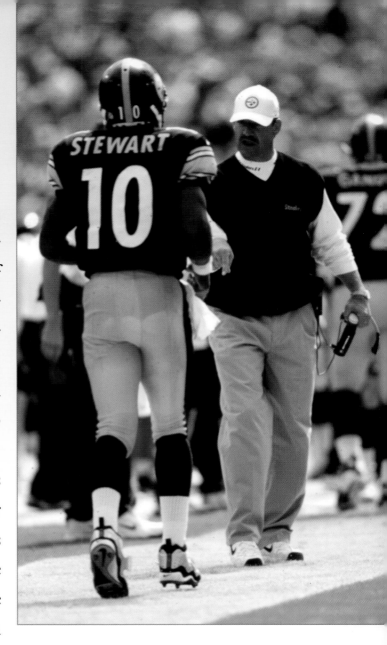

Bill Cowher offers words of advice to quarterback Kordell Stewart.

was constantly plugging holes in his lineup. Yet season after season, Pittsburgh was one of the NFL's best teams. Cowher guided the Steelers to the Super Bowl in 1996, but they lost. Nine years later, he delivered Pittsburgh's fifth championship in Super Bowl XL.

Pittsburgh's next two trips to the Super Bowl came under coach Mike Tomlin. He was similar to Noll and built the Steelers into a top defensive team. Tomlin was just 36 when he won Super Bowl XLIII—younger than any Super Bowl coach in history. He also became the first African-American coach to win an NFL championship.

One Great Day

When the Steelers met the Indianapolis Colts in the 2006 playoffs, everyone knew what was at stake. The winner would get to play the Denver Broncos for a chance to advance to Super Bowl XL. The loser would go home. Most experts picked the Colts to win. They were playing in front of their own fans on their own field.

The Steelers needed to play a near-perfect game, and they did. They made very few mistakes and seized the rare opportunities the Colts gave them. With less than two minutes left, Pittsburgh clung to a 21–18 lead.

With the ball on the Indianapolis 2-yard line, Ben Roethlisberger called a running play for Jerome Bettis. He was almost unstoppable at moments like this. Bettis tried to crash across the goal line for a touchdown. Linebacker Gary Brackett made a hard tackle, and the ball popped loose. Safety Nick Harper scooped up the fumble and began racing toward the opposite end zone. Pittsburgh's dream

of reaching the Super Bowl had suddenly turned into a nightmare!

Roethlisberger made a desperate attempt to stop Harper. He reached out with his right hand and tried to trip him up. Harper stumbled and fell to the turf. Pittsburgh's young quarterback had prevented the game-winning touchdown. Moments later, the Colts lined up for a **field goal** to tie the game. They missed the kick, and the Steelers won.

Bettis, who planned to retire after the season, was the happiest person on the field. He did not want to be remembered as the player who cost his team a trip to the Super Bowl. "Great play," said a relieved Bettis after the game. "Ben made a great play."

LEFT: Jerome Bettis and Ben Roethlisberger celebrate their victory over the Indianapolis Colts.   **ABOVE**: Roethlisberger makes his game-saving tackle.

Legend Has It

John Stallworth

Which team had the best draft day in history?

LEGEND HAS IT that the Steelers did. Heading into the 1974 NFL draft, no one expected the Steelers to do anything special. The team had the 21st pick in each round, and it did not have a third-round pick at all. But as the draft progressed, one good player after another became available. Four of the team's first five selections were Lynn Swann, Jack Lambert, John Stallworth, and Mike Webster. No one knew it at the time, but not only did they all become stars, all four ended up in the **Hall of Fame**!

ABOVE: John Stallworth   **RIGHT**: Hines Ward

Who was the Steelers' best dancer?

LEGEND HAS IT that Hines Ward was. And he's got the trophy to prove it! In 2011, Ward teamed with Kym Johnson to compete on the television show *Dancing with the Stars*. Ward and Johnson did the *samba* for their final dance and received perfect 10s from all three judges to become champions.

Who was the Steelers' greatest triple threat?

LEGEND HAS IT that Bill Dudley was. The Steelers have had several do-it-all stars, including Kordell Stewart, who was an exciting quarterback, runner, and receiver in the 1990s. However, Dudley's performance in 1946 has never been matched. That season, he led the NFL with 604 rushing yards, 10 interceptions, and 14.2 yards per punt return.

Pittsburgh fans had a lot to be happy about after the 1972 season. The Steelers won 11 games and made it to the playoffs for the first time in 10 years. No one was sure whether they could beat the mighty Oakland Raiders at home in the first round. But win or lose, it had been an amazing year.

It was about to get more amazing. Late in the fourth quarter, the Steelers were winning 6–0. Nothing the Raiders tried seemed to work. Finally, with time running out, Oakland quarterback Ken Stabler tucked the ball under his arm and made a great run through the Pittsburgh defense for a touchdown. The Raiders now led with less than a minute left. The fans in Three Rivers Stadium were heartbroken.

The Steelers got the ball back and hoped to move into position to try a field goal. But their drive stalled on their own 40-yard line. Pittsburgh had time for one last play. Terry Bradshaw dropped back to pass, spotted John Fuqua open in the middle of the field, and launched the ball to him. Jack Tatum of the Raiders moved over to stop the play.

Franco Harris always receives a warm welcome from Steelers fans when he returns to Pittsburgh.

Tatum, Fuqua, and Bradshaw's pass came together at the same moment, and the ball ricocheted high into the air. Everyone stopped for an instant, thinking the game was over. But rookie Franco Harris kept going. He caught the ball just before it hit the ground and ran 42 yards for the game-winning touchdown!

According to the rules at that time, Harris's touchdown would not have counted had the ball bounced off Fuqua. Did the Pittsburgh receiver touch the ball last, or did Tatum? The officials ruled that it was a "clean" catch—the touchdown counted. The play went down in history as the "Immaculate Reception."

Team Spirit

Pittsburgh fans call themselves "Steeler Nation" and take great pride in supporting their team. Many bring their "Terrible Towels" to home games. They wave them to inspire the Steelers and distract the other team.

Tailgate parties are another fun tradition for Steelers fans. They serve foods famous in Pittsburgh, including sausage and peppers, chipped ham barbecue sandwiches, pierogies, and kielbasa and sauerkraut. People also make their own versions of a "Roethlis Burger,"

which is a hamburger prepared in honor of Ben Roethlisberger.

Steelers fans unite in song as well. Their two favorites are "Here We Go!" and the "Steelers Polka." No one has ever sung them with more pride than Tom Santucci. Before the Steelers played in Super Bowl XLV, he painted his house black and gold. It quickly became one of Pittsburgh's most famous *landmarks*.

LEFT: A fan shows off her Terrible Towel.
ABOVE: The Roethlis Burger is a mouthful—and then some!

n this timeline, each Super Bowl is listed under the year it was played. Remember that the Super Bowl is held early in the year and is actually part of the previous season. For example, Super Bowl XLVI was played on February 5, 2012, but it was the championship of the 2011 NFL season.

1940
The team changes its name to Steelers.

1960
Bobby Layne becomes the NFL's all-time passing leader.

1933
Art Rooney starts the team as the Pirates.

1946
Bill Dudley is named NFL MVP.

1975
The Steelers win Super Bowl IX.

Art Rooney is shown dressed in white in this team photo of the Pirates.

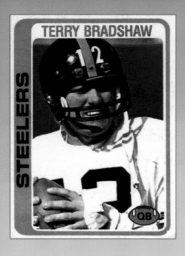

Terry Bradshaw was a two-time Super Bowl MVP.

Santonio Holmes made the winning catch in Super Bowl XLIII.

1980
The Steelers win Super Bowl XIV.

2006
The Steelers win Super Bowl XL.

2009
The Steelers win their sixth Super Bowl.

1992
Barry Foster sets a team record with 1,690 rushing yards.

2011
Hines Ward catches the 1,000th pass of his career.

LaMarr Woodley was a key player for the 2009 champs.

A TRUE VETERAN

After his first season with Pittsburgh, running back Rocky Bleier was drafted into the army and sent to Vietnam. He was wounded in both legs but returned to the Steelers and rushed for more than 1,000 yards in 1976.

MAKING THEM COUNT

In a 2009 game against the Green Bay Packers, rookie Mike Wallace caught two passes. The first was a 60-yard touchdown on the first play of the game. The second was also a touchdown—a game-winner on Pittsburgh's final play.

AD MEN

In 2010, Troy Polamalu starred in a series of shampoo commercials. They were so popular that the company insured his hair for $1 million. Polamalu followed in the footsteps of Joe Greene. He won an award for his performance in a Coca-Cola commercial from the 1970s.

FACE FACTS

Bobby Layne, who played quarterback for the Steelers from 1958 to 1962, was one of the last men in the NFL to play without a facemask.

GOING WILD

Ben Roethlisberger was once asked what he would choose if he could have any pet in the world. He said it was a tie between a monkey, a dolphin, and a white tiger.

SMART GUY

In 1938, Pittsburgh rookie Byron "Whizzer" White led the NFL in rushing yards. He then quit to study at world-famous Oxford University in England. During World War II, White became friendly with a Navy officer named John F. Kennedy. Kennedy was elected president of the United States in 1960. He later appointed White to the *Supreme Court*.

LEFT: Troy Polamalu   **ABOVE**: Bobby Layne

Joe Greene

"Going after the quarterback is like playing king of the mountain. When you get the quarterback, you're on top of the mountain."

▶ *Joe Greene, on what it feels like to tackle the quarterback*

"Before you win a game, you have to not lose it."

▶ *Chuck Noll, on the importance of limiting mistakes*

"I may not be the flashiest wide receiver out there. But I get the job done for my team."

▶ *Hines Ward, on why he was such a favorite of Steelers fans*

"The only way to shut everybody up is to win."

▶ *Terry Bradshaw, on how he dealt with criticism as a player*

"Guys like Ben? **Competitors**? Playing football is like breathing to them."

▶ *Mike Tomlin, on Ben Roethlisberger*

"I've been able to do some **extraordinary** things in an ordinary body—but I'm not an ordinary guy."

▶ *Jerome Bettis, on being one of football's biggest running backs*

"Chuck and I hit it off the first day we met. We had an argument!"

▶ *Art Rooney, on his favorite coach, Chuck Noll*

"The game is designed to reward the ones who hit the hardest. If you can't take it, you shouldn't play."

▶ *Jack Lambert, on why he was such a fierce tackler*

LEFT: Joe Greene   **ABOVE**: Mike Tomlin

Great Debates

People who root for the Steelers love to compare their favorite moments, teams, and players. Some debates have been going on for years! How would you settle these classic football arguments?

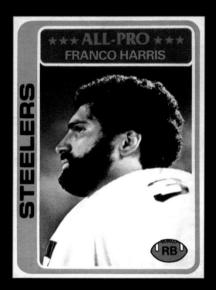

★★★ ALL-PRO ★★★
FRANCO HARRIS
STEELERS
RB

The Immaculate Reception in the 1972 playoffs was the greatest play in Steelers history ...

... because no NFL team has ever come so close to losing a **postseason** game and ended up winning it. Franco Harris (LEFT) showed how great he was by not giving up on the play. His amazing catch shocked everyone watching the game. More than 40 years later, people still remember it!

That was a lucky play. The catch by Santonio Holmes to win Super Bowl XLII was the greatest ...

... because it took incredible skill and also gave the Steelers their sixth championship. Holmes had to keep both feet in bounds while the rest of his body was flying out of bounds. If he dropped the ball, the Steelers might have gone home losers. As for the Immaculate Reception, people forget that Pittsburgh lost a week later and didn't make it to the Super Bowl that year.

Barry Foster had the greatest season of any Pittsburgh running back in 1992 ...

... because he set the team record with 1,690 rushing yards. Foster was a powerful back who ran like a runaway train. Unfortunately, his career was cut short by an injury. In 1992, he was the entire Pittsburgh offense. The Steelers struggled in the passing game, so opponents focused on stopping Foster. He still managed to finish second in the league in rushing.

What about the Bus? Jerome Bettis had a better season in 1997 ...

... because every time the Steelers handed him the ball, they knew he'd get the yards they needed. Bettis (RIGHT, on the cover of *Sports Illustrated*) blew through holes and crashed through tackles to gain 1,665 yards in 1997. The only reason that he didn't break Foster's record was that the Steelers rested him in the final game of the season. They had already made the playoffs and wanted

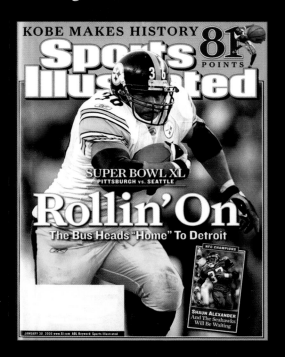

him as fresh as possible for the postseason. If the Bus had taken the field, he would have rolled right by Foster.

The great Steelers teams and players have left their marks on the record books. These are the "best of the best" …

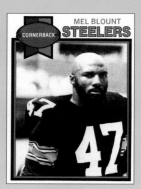

Mel Blount

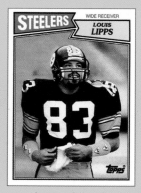

Louis Lipps

STEELERS AWARD WINNERS

WINNER	AWARD	YEAR
Bill Dudley	NFL Most Valuable Player	1946
Franco Harris	Offensive Rookie of the Year	1972
Joe Greene	Defensive Player of the Year	1972
Joe Greene	Defensive Player of the Year	1974
Jack Lambert	Defensive Rookie of the Year	1974
Mel Blount	Defensive Player of the Year	1975
Franco Harris	Super Bowl IX MVP	1975
Lynn Swann	Super Bowl X MVP	1976
Jack Lambert	Defensive Player of the Year	1976
Terry Bradshaw	NFL Most Valuable Player	1978
Terry Bradshaw	Super Bowl XIII MVP	1979
Terry Bradshaw	Super Bowl XIV MVP	1980
Louis Lipps	Rookie of the Year	1984
John Stallworth	Comeback Player of the Year	1984
Bill Cowher	Coach of the Year	1992
Rod Woodson	Defensive Player of the Year	1993
Jerome Bettis	Comeback Player of the Year	1996
Kendrell Bell	Defensive Rookie of the Year	2001
Tommy Maddox	Comeback Player of the Year	2002
Ben Roethlisberger	Offensive Rookie of the Year	2004
Hines Ward	Super Bowl XL MVP	2006
James Harrison	Defensive Player of the Year	2008
Santonio Holmes	Super Bowl XLIII MVP	2009
Troy Polamalu	Defensive Player of the Year	2010

STEELERS ACHIEVEMENTS

ACHIEVEMENT	YEAR
AFC Champions	1974
Super Bowl IX Champions	1974*
AFC Champions	1975
Super Bowl X Champions	1975*
AFC Champions	1978
Super Bowl XIII Champions	1978*
AFC Champions	1979
Super Bowl XIV Champions	1979*
AFC Champions	1995
AFC Champions	2005
Super Bowl XL Champions	2005*
AFC Champions	2008
Super Bowl XLIII Champions	2008*
AFC Champions	2010

* Super Bowls are played early the following year, but the game is counted as the championship of this season.

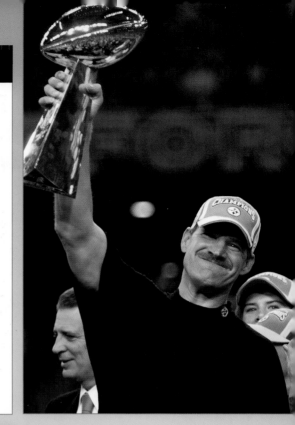

ABOVE: Bill Cowher raises the Super Bowl trophy.
LEFT: Owner Dan Rooney is interviewed after Super Bowl XLIII.

Pinpoints

The history of a football team is made up of many smaller stories. These stories take place all over the map—not just in the city a team calls "home." Match the pushpins on these maps to the **Team Facts**, and you will begin to see the story of the Steelers unfold!

TEAM FACTS

1 Pittsburgh, Pennsylvania—*The Steelers have played here since 1933.*

2 Detroit, Michigan—*The Steelers won Super Bowl XL here.*

3 Lima, Ohio—*Ben Roethlisberger was born here.*

4 Fort Dix, New Jersey—*Franco Harris was born here.*

5 Alcoa, Tennessee—*Lynn Swann was born here.*

6 Stockton, Kansas—*Dale Dodrill was born here.*

7 Temple, Texas—*Joe Greene was born here.*

8 New Orleans, Louisiana—*The Steelers won their first Super Bowl here.*

9 Tampa, Florida—*The Steelers won their sixth Super Bowl here.*

10 Pasadena, California—*The Steelers won Super Bowl XIV here.*

11 Prienzing, Germany—*Ernie Stautner was born here.*

12 Seoul, South Korea—*Hines Ward was born here.*

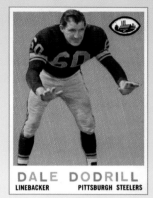

Dale Dodrill

45

Glossary

🏈 **ALL-AROUND**—Good at many different parts of the game.

🏈 **ALL-PRO**—An honor given to the best players at their position at the end of each season.

🧠 *COMPETITORS*—People with a strong desire to win.

🧠 *CONCUSSION*—A head injury that affects the brain.

🏈 **DRAFT**—Select from a group of the best college players. The NFL draft is held each spring.

🧠 *DYNASTY*—A family, group, or team that maintains power over time.

🧠 *ELUSIVE*—Difficult to catch.

🧠 *ERA*—A period of time in history.

🧠 *EXTRAORDINARY*—Unusual, or unusually talented.

🏈 **FIELD GOAL**—A goal from the field, kicked over the crossbar and between the goal posts. A field goal is worth three points.

🧠 *GENERATIONS*—Periods of years roughly equal to the time it takes for a person to be born, grow up, and have children.

🧠 *GREAT DEPRESSION*—The economic crisis that started in 1929 and lasted until the 1940s.

🏈 **HALL OF FAME**—The museum in Canton, Ohio, where football's greatest players are honored.

🧠 *INSPIRATIONAL*—The ability to give positive and confident feelings to others.

🏈 **INTERCEPTION**—A pass that is caught by the defensive team.

🧠 *LANDMARKS*—Notable places that people like to visit.

🏈 **LINE OF SCRIMMAGE**—The imaginary line that separates the offense and defense before each play begins.

🧠 *LOGO*—A symbol or design that represents a company or team.

🏈 **MOST VALUABLE PLAYER (MVP)**—The award given each year to the league's best player; also given to the best player in the Super Bowl and Pro Bowl.

🏈 **NATIONAL FOOTBALL LEAGUE (NFL)**—The league that started in 1920 and is still operating today.

🧠 *PHILOSOPHY*—A theory of how things should work.

🏈 **PLAYOFFS**—The games played after the regular season to determine which teams play in the Super Bowl.

🏈 **POSTSEASON**—Another term for playoffs.

🧠 *PROFESSIONAL*—A player or team that plays a sport for money.

🏈 **ROOKIE**—A player in his first season.

🧠 *SAMBA*—A dance popular in Brazil.

🏈 **SUPER BOWL**—The championship of the NFL, played between the winners of the National Football Conference and American Football Conference.

🧠 *SUPREME COURT*—The highest court in the United States.

🧠 *TRADITION*—A belief or custom that is handed down from generation to generation.

🧠 *VETERAN*—Having great experience.

🧠 *WORLD WAR II*—The war among the major powers of Europe, Asia, and North America that lasted from 1939 to 1945. The United States entered the war in 1941.

OVERTIME

TEAM SPIRIT introduces a great way to stay up to date with your team! Visit our **OVERTIME** link and get connected to the latest and greatest updates. **OVERTIME** serves as a young reader's ticket to an exclusive web page—with more stories, fun facts, team records, and photos of the Steelers. Content is updated during and after each season. The **OVERTIME** feature also enables readers to send comments and letters to the author!

Log onto:

www.norwoodhousepress.com/library.aspx

and click on the tab: **TEAM SPIRIT** to access **OVERTIME**.

Read all the books in the series to learn more about professional sports. For a complete listing of the baseball, basketball, football, and hockey teams in the **TEAM SPIRIT** series, visit our website at:

www.norwoodhousepress.com/library.aspx

On the Road

PITTSBURGH STEELERS
100 Art Rooney Avenue
Pittsburgh, Pennsylvania 15212
412-432-7800
www.steelers.com

THE PRO FOOTBALL HALL OF FAME
2121 George Halas Drive NW
Canton, Ohio 44708
330-456-8207
www.profootballhof.com

On the Bookshelf

To learn more about the sport of football, look for these books at your library or bookstore:

- Frederick, Shane. *The Best of Everything Football Book.* North Mankato, Minnesota: Capstone Press, 2011.

- Jacobs, Greg. *The Everything Kids' Football Book: The All-Time Greats, Legendary Teams, Today's Superstars—And Tips on Playing Like a Pro.* Avon, Massachusetts: Adams Media Corporation, 2010.

- Editors of *Sports Illustrated for Kids. 1st and 10: Top 10 Lists of Everything in Football.* New York, New York: Sports Illustrated Books, 2011.

Index

PAGE NUMBERS IN **BOLD** REFER TO ILLUSTRATIONS.

About the Author

MARK STEWART has written more than 50 books on football and over 150 sports books for kids. He grew up in New York City during the 1960s rooting for the Giants and Jets, and was lucky enough to meet players from both teams. Mark comes from a family of writers. His grandfather was Sunday Editor of *The New York Times,* and his mother was Articles Editor of *Ladies' Home Journal* and *McCall's.* Mark has profiled hundreds of athletes over the past 25 years. He has also written several books about his native New York and New Jersey, his home today. Mark is a graduate of Duke University, with a degree in history. He lives and works in a home overlooking Sandy Hook, New Jersey. You can contact Mark through the Norwood House Press website.